Teddy Takes a Vacation:

The Story of the Real Teddy Bear

by Kate Chase

illustrated by Doug Knutson

Orlando Boston Dallas Chicago San Diego

Visit *The Learning Site!*

www.harcourtschool.com

President Teddy Roosevelt needed a vacation. He had been President for a year, and that is a hard job. Teddy's friends knew Teddy would enjoy a vacation in the woods.

Teddy's friends invited him to join them on a bear hunt. The President enjoyed the outdoors, from the plains to the woods. He helped set up many parks in the United States. Teddy was happy to take a vacation and relax.

Teddy Goes on a Vacation

Teddy and his friends went to the woods for two days. There was no noise there. The woods were green and quiet. The bears were quiet, too. The hunters couldn't find any.

Teddy's friends began to worry. They had told the President that there were many bears in the woods. They did not want his trip to be spoiled. They came up with a plan.

The President's friends found a bear. It was an old and tired one. Teddy's friends captured it so the President would have a bear to shoot.

Teddy Won't Shoot

Teddy's friends pointed out the bear. The President showed his manners and thanked them. Then he made his choice. He said it would not be fair to shoot a captured bear.

Teddy told his friends, “If I shot that helpless fellow, I wouldn’t be able to look my boys in the eyes again.” He didn’t shoot the bear. He felt sorry for it.

The story of the President and the bear was a good news story. An artist for a newspaper drew Teddy and the bear. His picture showed a cute bear tied up. His picture showed the President saying he would not shoot the bear.

Newspaper readers loved the drawing. Soon lots of people knew the story. Friends told the artist he should sell the idea to a toy company. The artist would not. Everyone knew about that bear, though.

In New York, a man named Morris Michtom and his wife had a store. They sold candy and toys. Morris saw the drawing of the President and the bear. He liked what the President did.

Morris's wife, Rose, made two toy bears. She used her imagination. Other toy bears were made to look like real bears. Rose made these two new bears soft and cute. The bears had black button eyes, and they could sit down.

The Teddy Bear Is Born

Rose and Morris put the bears in the window of their store. They asked the President if they could use his name. He said yes. They called the bears "Teddy's bears."

The soft, new bears were a real joy to children. They were such a hit that the Michtoms had to make more and more. The family began to make and sell bears all over.

Soon, the Michtoms started a toy company to make bears. By 1906, every boy and girl wanted a teddy bear. The President even used a toy bear when he ran for President again. (He won.)

Today, teddy bears ride in cars. They dress up in outfits. You can find a matador teddy bear and firefighter teddy bear. Almost every child has a teddy bear, the bear that President Roosevelt would not shoot.